HULU

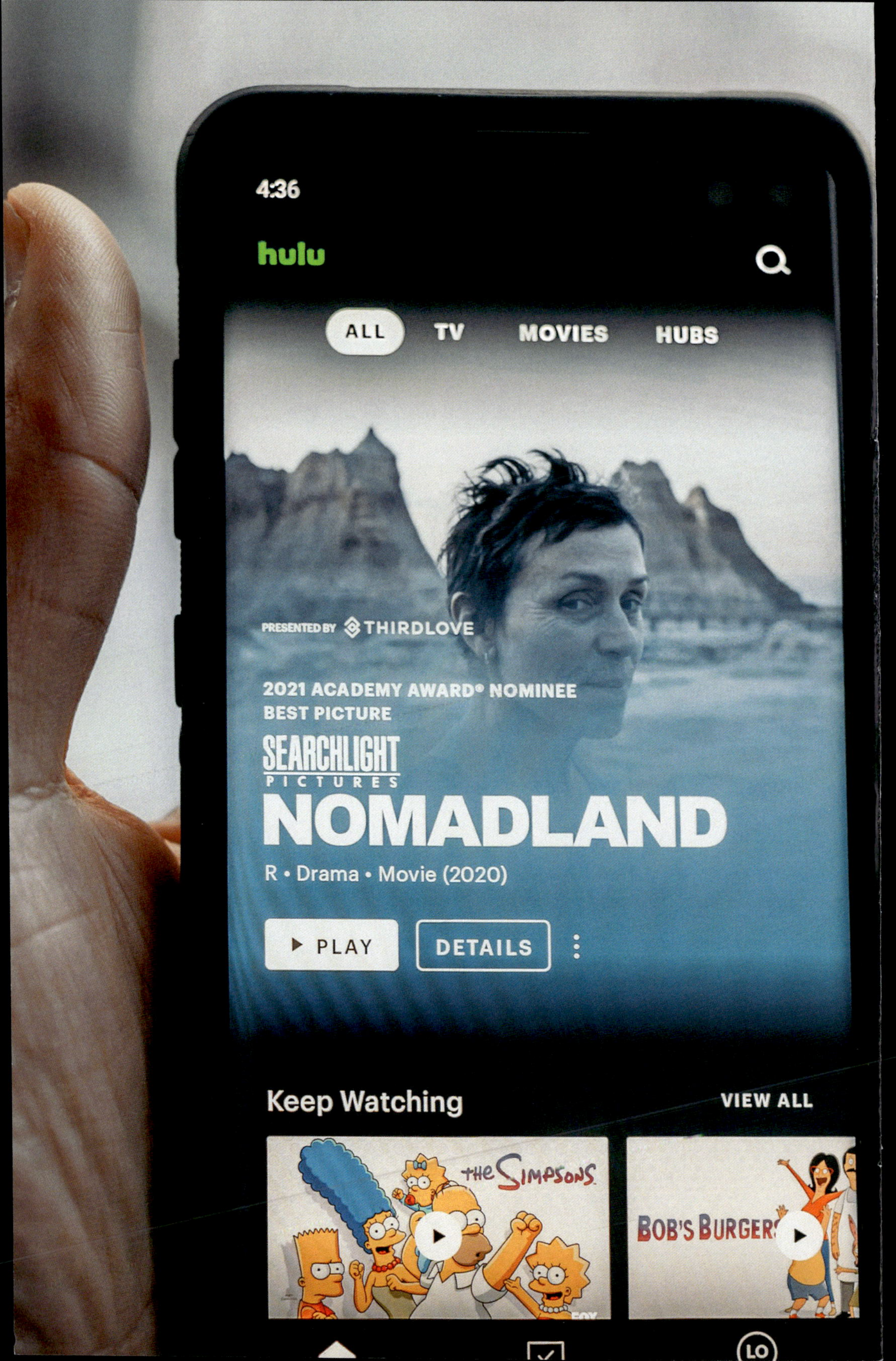
4:36
hulu
ALL
TV
MOVIES
HUBS
PRESENTED BY THIRDLOVE
2021 ACADEMY AWARD® NOMINEE
BEST PICTURE
SEARCHLIGHT PICTURES
NOMADLAND
R • Drama • Movie (2020)
PLAY
DETAILS
Keep Watching
VIEW ALL
THE SIMPSONS
BOB'S BURGERS

HULU

ODYSSEYS

RACHAEL HANEL

CREATIVE EDUCATION · CREATIVE PAPERBACKS

Published by Creative Education and Creative Paperbacks
P.O. Box 227, Mankato, Minnesota 56002
Creative Education and Creative Paperbacks are imprints of
The Creative Company
www.thecreativecompany.us

Design by Blue Design
Art direction by Graham Morgan

Images by Getty Images/AaronP/Bauer-Griffin, 63, Angela Weiss, 48, CHRIS DELMAS, 6, Dia Dipasupil, 44, Filippo Arteconi, 64, Jason LaVeris, 11, Kevin Winter, 8, Kimimasa Mayama/Bloomberg, 34–35, Michael Buckner/Variety, 70–71, Todd Williamson, 39; Hulu, cover, 60, 69, 72; Pexels/freestocks.org, 56, Pixabay, 40, Quang Nguyen Vinh, 26, Ron Lach, 75, Steve Johnson, 4–5; Unsplash/BoliviaInteligente, 29, Bruno Guerrero, 19, Darren Gundling, 30, Matthew Sanchez, 24, National Library of Medicine, 16, Phillip Goldsberry, 51, Tech Daily, 2, 12, 52, 66, Yasmina H, 59; Wikimedia Commons/Gage Skidmore, 20

Library of Congress Cataloging-in-Publication Data
Names: Hanel, Rachael author
Title: Hulu / Rachael Hanel.
Description: Mankato, Minnesota : Creative Education and Creative Paperbacks, [2026] | Series: Odysseys in business | Includes bibliographical references and index. | Audience: Ages 12-15 | Audience: Grades 7-9 | Summary: “Explore Hulu’s transformative role in streaming entertainment. Learn how it blends original storytelling with innovation, captivating audiences and inspiring high-school age storytellers to redefine media. This title includes sidebars, a glossary, selected bibliography, websites, and an index”— Provided by publisher.
Identifiers: LCCN 2025021207 (print) | LCCN 2025021208 (ebook) | ISBN 9798895811344 library binding | ISBN 9798896800873 paperback | ISBN 9798895812600 ebook
Subjects: LCSH: Hulu (Firm)— Juvenile literature | Streaming video— United States— Juvenile literature | Television broadcasting--United States— Juvenile literature | Subscription television--United States— Juvenile literature
Classification: LCC HD9697.V544 H8543 2026 (print) | LCC HD9697.V544 (ebook) | DDC 384.55/54--dc23/eng/20250530
LC record available at https://lccn.loc.gov/2025021207
LC ebook record available at https://lccn.loc.gov/2025021208

Printed in the United States

hulu

CONTENTS

PRIMETIME
EMMYS
OUTSTANDING
DRAMA SERIES

Introduction

On stage at the 69th Primetime Emmy Awards, talk show host and actor, Oprah Winfrey, held an envelope. She was there to announce the night's biggest award: Outstanding Drama Series. The audience was silent. Everyone seemed to hold their breath. Then Winfrey opened the envelope, looked up, and practically screamed, "*The Handmaid's Tale*!"

OPPOSITE: Actor Elisabeth Moss (R) accepts Outstanding Drama Series for 'The Handmaid's Tale' from Oprah Winfrey onstage during the 69th Annual Primetime Emmy Awards.

Ripples of shock and amazement swept through the crowd. No one was more amazed than executives at Hulu, which produced *The Handmaid's Tale*. It was on this night that Hulu made history. It became the first **streaming** service to win an Emmy for Outstanding Drama Series. Even more amazing, it beat out three other nominated shows from its rival, Netflix. As Jack Koblin wrote in *The New York Times,* "It was inevitable that a streaming service would win an Emmy for best drama at some point, but no one expected Hulu to get there first."

This was not the show's only win that night. Other winners included Elisabeth Moss for best actress, Ann Dowd for best supporting actress, Reed Morano for outstanding director, and Bruce Miller for writing. Hulu was only ten years old, but it was clearly becoming a major player in the streaming wars.

Cast of *The Handmaid's Tale* at the 69th Emmy Awards

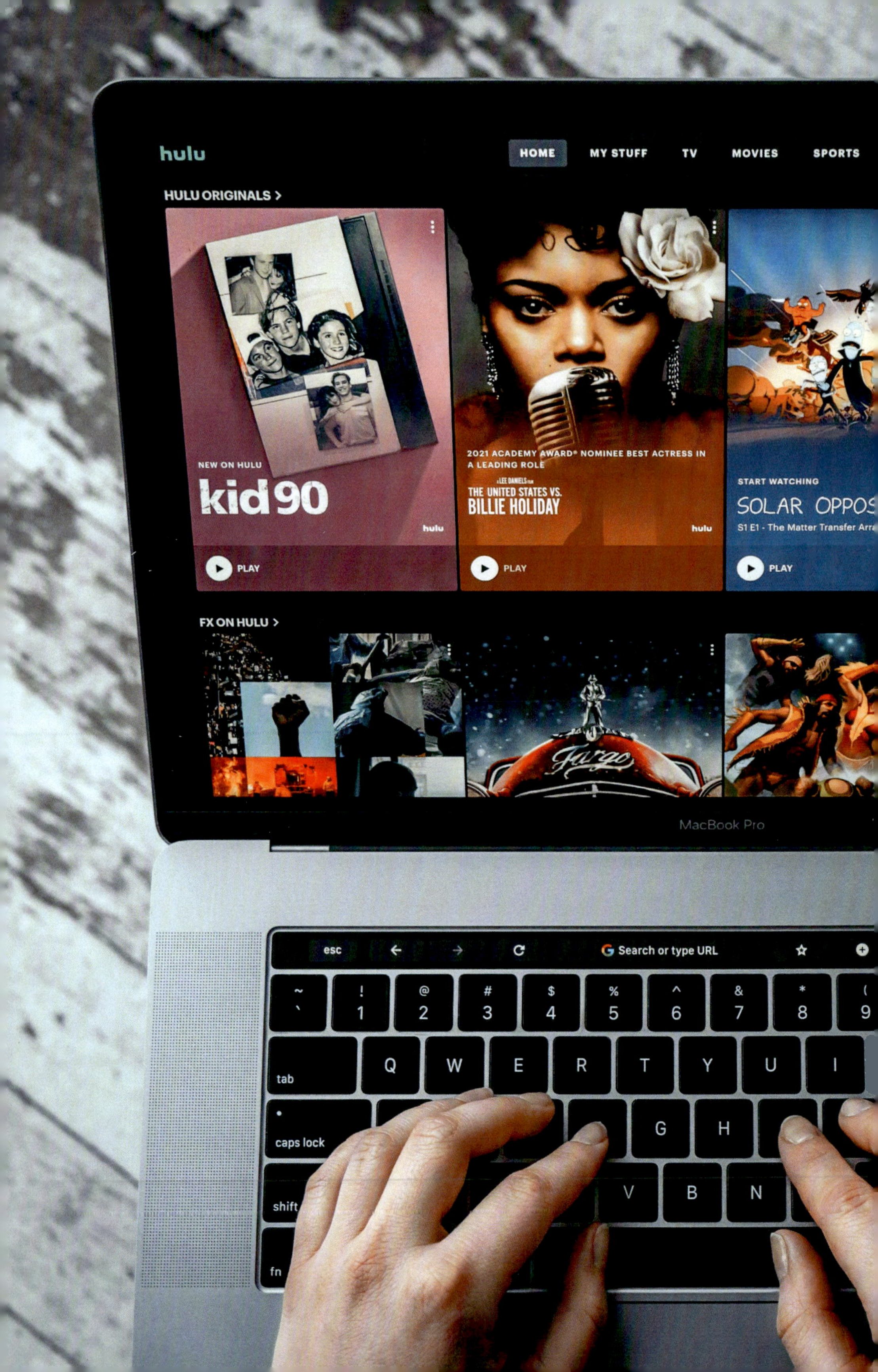
hulu
HOME
MY STUFF
TV
MOVIES
SPORTS
HULU ORIGINALS >
NEW ON HULU
kid 90
hulu
PLAY
2021 ACADEMY AWARD® NOMINEE BEST ACTRESS IN A LEADING ROLE
THE UNITED STATES VS. BILLIE HOLIDAY
hulu
PLAY
START WATCHING
PLAY
FX ON HULU >
Fargo
MacBook Pro
esc
Search or type URL
tab
caps lock
shift
fn

A New Way to Watch TV

Watching our favorite shows and movies on computers, tablets, or phones feels normal now. We're used to turning on the TV, opening a streaming app, and scrolling through a menu. But before Hulu changed everything in 2008, watching TV was very different.

OPPOSITE: Streaming services such as Hulu changed the way people thought about television.

For decades, TV programs aired at a specific time, and viewers gathered in front of their television sets to watch their favorites. By the 1980s, **video cassette recorders** (VCRs) allowed people to record shows for later viewing, and in the 1990s, **digital video recorders** (DVRs) served a similar purpose. Still, most people watched shows live as they aired.

People could watch TV in several ways. One option was to buy a television **antenna**, which receives **broadcast** airwaves. **Broadcast networks**—such as ABC, CBS, NBC,

"FOR DECADES, TV PROGRAMS AIRED AT A SPECIFIC TIME, AND VIEWERS GATHERED IN FRONT OF THEIR TELEVISION SETS TO WATCH THEIR FAVORITES."

Fox, and PBS are considered public service channels because they offer important information like local news and emergency notices along with entertainment programming, including sitcoms, dramas, and reality shows. Because these channels serve the public good and are free to access with just a television set and an antenna,

OPPOSITE In the 1960s and '70s, most U.S. households had just a few TV channels.

they remained the most popular delivery method for television programming well into the late 20th century.

By the 1980s, however, broadcast networks faced new competition. **Satellites** could beam in programs as long as a household had a satellite dish to receive the signals. **Cable** companies used underground cables to transmit TV programs into homes. Viewers liked satellite and cable television because many more programs were available. Networks like ESPN, MTV, and Comedy Central gained huge followings. But unlike broadcast networks, people had to pay for these channels. On top of regular satellite and cable packages available, viewers could also subscribe to premium networks like HBO and Showtime. These networks aired almost-new movies and **original programming**.

The way people watched movies began to shift around the 1980s. In the United States, movie theater attendance had been in decline since the 1930s, and the advent of television in the 1950s led more households to enjoy entertainment at home. The introduction of the VCR in the 1980s further enabled viewers to rent movies from video stores and watch them on their own schedule. In 1997, Netflix revolutionized the experience by renting **digital video discs** (DVDs) by mail, eliminating the need to step out for a rental.

A decade later, in March 2007, a mysterious announcement made waves: a new company was about to offer an unheard-of option for watching TV shows and movies—streaming them directly through an internet-connected computer. Hulu, the name of this new venture,

VCRs allowed viewers to rent and collect movies to watch on their own time.

First Commerical

"Hello Earth. I'm Alec Baldwin, TV star."

With those words, tens of millions of people learned about Hulu for the first time. The company spent millions of dollars to air a commercial during Super Bowl XLIII on February 1, 2009. Hulu was just a few months old. It had just a few thousand users. Baldwin told viewers they could watch their favorite TV shows anytime, anywhere, for free. People could watch TV shows without a television set? It was a wild, new idea. The Super Bowl ad was the perfect time for Hulu to tell the world what it could do.

attracted attention with its **tagline**, "Watch your favorites. Anytime. Anywhere."

At the time of the announcement, the average household had been able to access the internet for about a decade. But the first internet connections through a dial-up **modem** were slow. However, the technology quickly improved. By 2007, internet speeds could support the large amounts of data needed to stream TV shows and movies.

Before Hulu, users had only a couple of options for streaming, on-demand internet content. YouTube offered millions of videos, but very little television or movie options. YouTube featured mostly **user-generated content**, which often lacked quality. And Netflix had just started to branch out from its DVD rental business and offered subscribers some limited streaming programming.

Hulu formed as a partnership between two large media companies that already were producing television shows and movies: NBC Universal and News Corp.

“BEFORE HULU, USERS HAD ONLY A COUPLE OF OPTIONS FOR STREAMING, ON-DEMAND INTERNET CONTENT.”

NBC Universal owned the broadcast network NBC. It owned cable networks such as Bravo and USA. It also owned Universal Studios, which produced popular movie franchises like *The Fast and the Furious*. News Corp. owned the Fox broadcast network and cable networks like FX and National Geographic. They also owned a movie studio—21st Century Fox. The founders of Hulu saw enormous potential in finding new ways to offer their already existing TV and movie options to viewers.

30 Rockefeller Plaza, NBCUniversal's headquarters

Launching this new venture required money. Even though NBC Universal and News Corp. were huge companies, they needed investment from an outside partner. Providence Equity Partners provided an initial investment of $100 million dollars in exchange for a 10 percent ownership in the company.

But after that announcement in March 2007, no one heard anything for six months. It was as if the whole venture just disappeared. In fact, many media industry experts thought the deal had fallen through. However,

Hulu Gets its Name

Hulu comes from the Mandarin language. It has two meanings. For one, it literally translates to "gourd," something with a hard shell that can be carved out. In that way, it can hold important items. Hulu's founding CEO, Jason Kilar, said he liked that meaning. He saw Hulu as a service that held important entertainment options for viewers. Another meaning is "interactive recording," which seems highly relevant to a streaming service.

In October, Hulu quietly launched a beta version with fewer than 1,000 handpicked users, who could then invite others. Soon, thousands were discovering everything Hulu had to offer. And in the beginning, it was a lot.

Hulu offered 83 television shows, including *Family Guy*, *The Simpsons*, and *Heroes*. It streamed current and older TV shows that aired on channels owned by NBC Universal and News Corp. Many of the current TV shows aired on Hulu as soon as the next day. The movie options were more limited. Only 10 movies were available in those early days. But the number of movie options quickly grew.

The best part about this new service? It was entirely free to use. Hulu made money by selling ads. Viewers had to sit through brief commercials lasting 5 to 30 seconds.

The gamble of starting a company that offered an entirely new way of watching TV and movies paid off. Within one year of its launch, Hulu was the second-most popular site for videos, behind only the giant YouTube.

The first couple of years were so wildly successful that the company attracted the attention of a very big, very popular potential partner: Disney.

In 2009, Disney became a partner in Hulu by acquiring a 27.5% stake—equal to the stakes held by NBC Universal and News Corp—with the remaining ownership split between Providence Equity Partners and Hulu staff. Disney's involvement allowed Hulu to stream ABC shows, giving it access to content from three of the four major U.S. broadcast networks (NBC, Fox, and ABC). The partnership also enabled Hulu to use Disney's extensive catalog of popular movies dating back decades.

Even with all the new shows and movies, Hulu was still free to use. However, Disney's involvement increased the platform's scale—and with that, its operating costs. Shortly after Disney entered the picture, Hulu executives saw they could not pay their bills by selling advertisements alone.

"THE DECISION TO ASK SUBSCRIBERS TO PAY WAS NOT AN EASY ONE."

The decision to ask subscribers to pay was not an easy one. The battle was between Hulu's owners and advertisers. The owners wanted to make more money, so the solution seemed simple. But advertisers feared once Hulu asked customers to pay, they would choose to leave the service instead. Advertisers prefer free content because it attracts more viewers.

In the end, Hulu's owners won out. In 2010, Hulu launched a subscription service called Hulu Plus. For

Hulu's CEO Jason Kilar in 2011

"THE LEADERSHIP TEAM HAD A NEW IDEA: CREATE ORIGINAL PROGRAMMING."

$10 per month, subscribers could enjoy Hulu content without ad interruptions.

Now that the company had built a solid subscriber base by offering TV shows and movies, the leadership team had a new idea: create original programming. In 2011, Hulu created brand-new content to attract new customers. Executives based this decision on a small number of web series that found success on Hulu, such as *The LXD: The Legion of Extraordinary Dancers*.

Some of the first original programs that aired on Hulu in 2011 and 2012 included the animated shows *Trailer Trash* and *The LeBrons*, as well as the action series *The Confession*.

The Disney partnership, the subscription model, and original programming paid off for Hulu by the middle of 2011. The subscription base grew to 875,000 customers. Those customers could choose from an eye-popping 2,180 TV series. In 2011, Hulu brought in $420 million dollars between subscriptions and advertising. By 2012,

OPPOSITE Actress Alexandra Rodriguez attends the Premiere Of Hulu's "East Los High Season 3.

the company pulled in $695 million and had 3 million Hulu Plus subscribers.

Despite these successes, Hulu experienced some turmoil behind the scenes. The three owners—Comcast (which had bought NBC Universal), News Corp, and Disney—looked into selling Hulu in 2013. But new ownership was hard to find. Even though the company had found success, it still was a baby in the business world at just five years old. The era of streaming was still relatively new. Ownership posed a

Hulu Latino

In 2011, Hulu launched Hulu Latino to expand its audience to Spanish-speaking viewers. Latino audiences were watching more streaming services at the end of 2013 compared to the year before. By 2014, Hulu Latino offered more than 100 programs in Spanish. Some of that programming was original. *East Los High* was a drama set in a high school that featured all Latino actors. Two reality shows, *Mi Vida en Sayulita* and *Los Cowboys*, were also filmed in Spanish. Hulu Latino also featured English-language shows with strong Latino themes and cast members.

129•125
HD

OPPOSITE The broadcast networks wanted to support Hulu without losing focus on traditional TV.

risk to investors. Who knew how long people would keep streaming TV shows and movies before something even better came along?

When no buyers stepped forward, Hulu's leaders committed to the business. They rounded up $750 million and invested in the future.

The ownership structure also posed a challenge. Now that Hulu accessed shows from all three major networks, competing interests emerged. The broadcast networks—

Fox NBC, and ABC—still had to focus on content for their broadcast audiences. But they also wanted to have enough content on Hulu to satisfy streaming audiences. They found themselves spread thin. Hulu marked a new frontier in how people watched TV. But all three companies still had a vested interest in traditional, broadcast television. It was difficult to do some things the old way while trying to adapt to new audiences.

Balancing interests in both traditional broadcasting and streaming posed additional problems for Providence,

The First Original Series

Battleground debuted on Hulu on February 14, 2012, becoming the company's first scripted series. Until that point, Hulu had aired previously filmed TV shows and movies. *Battleground* was a political comedy-drama set in Wisconsin. The storyline featured people working on a campaign to elect an unlikely candidate to the U.S. Senate. Network executives had passed on the project because they thought it was too political. *Battleground* soon opened the floodgates to a whole host of Hulu original programming.

Hulu's private investor. Its leadership recognized the vast potential of streaming services and urged the other owners to shift focus away from traditional broadcast audiences.

Amid these challenges, Hulu's CEO Jason Kilar ruffled some feathers of the leadership team. He publicly stated that the subscription price was too high and criticized traditional TV—a stance that clashed with board members still focused on broadcast audiences. Kilar's opinions aligned more closely with the

Jason Kilar

vision of Providence than with that of the traditional broadcasters.

Even with all of the conflict, toward the end of 2012, Hulu was adding subscribers more quickly than any other streaming service.

But it was clear that Kilar's vision was different from that of the company's owners. In March 2013, he left Hulu. This presented a do-or-die moment for the company. Would the massive investments the owners put in pay off? Or would it fail, like so many other **start-ups**?

Rapid Growth and Success

Hulu was poised for rapid expansion. In October 2013 the company named Mike Hopkins as its new CEO to usher in a period of growth. Hopkins was already familiar with Hulu, having served as an executive at Fox Networks Group—a division of News Corp—and as a board member since 2011.

When Hopkins assumed leadership, Hulu reached a major milestone by surpassing $1 billion in **revenue** and amassing 5 million subscribers. In a significant shift, more than half of these subscribers began watching Hulu programming on television—through devices such as Apple TV or gaming consoles. The streaming experience began to look more and more like the TV-watching experience of decades past.

But competition was stiff. Hulu still trailed behind the streaming powerhouses of Netflix and Amazon Prime. And new competitors popped up regularly. Devices that connected to televisions and streamed internet content grew increasingly popular. For example, in 2012 Roku, a leading streaming box, offered 800 channels, while smart devices like Apple TV came equipped with internet-ready apps. Meanwhile, major players entered

the market: Wal-Mart introduced Vudu, and Google backed YouTube and Google TV.

Hulu had to continue to find ways to set itself apart from its competition. Once again, it relied on its strength—a huge catalog of television shows. Soon, the

OPPOSITE New CEO Mike Hopkins and actress Mindy Kaling attend Hulu's *'The Mindy Project'* Season Four premiere.

company discovered another way to attract customers by reviving shows canceled by broadcast networks. For instance, after Fox **canceled** the fan-favorite *The Mindy Project* in 2015—a decision that might ordinarily have marked the end of the series—Hulu, of which Fox was a part owner, announced plans to stream a brand-new fourth season.

That same year, Hulu announced a major deal. It acquired the rights to stream episodes of *Seinfeld*, a hugely popular comedy that aired on NBC in the 1990s. Hulu reportedly paid an estimated $180 million for the streaming rights, which comes to roughly $1 million per episode. Hulu's competition, Netflix, had just bought the rights to air another massively popular 1990s comedy, *Friends*. The *Seinfeld* deal proved that Hulu had become a major player in the streaming wars.

The millions of subscribers to streaming services caught the attention of other large companies. In 2015, mobile phone providers saw streaming services as a way to at-

A Family Affair

When Hulu started in 2008, the idea was that people could watch TV shows and movies on their computers and mobile devices. But by 2015, Hulu executives noticed an interesting trend. More than half of Hulu viewers watched the service on television sets in their living rooms. In this way, the experience of watching Hulu was like watching TV in decades past. Viewers gathered with friends and family around a TV set to enjoy entertainment programming.

Smart phones offered a new way to access streaming services

tract customers. That year, T-Mobile offered a one-year free subscription to Hulu to new customers.

Subscription numbers continued to climb rapidly. By 2015, Hulu had reached 9 million subscribers and had recently introduced an ad-free plan priced at $12 per month—up from the $8 per month ad-supported option. Still, the company lagged far behind its rival, Netflix, which had 41 million subscribers.

Despite its growth and rising subscriber count, Hulu was losing money by 2015.

"CAST AND CREW NEED TO BE PAID, WITH ACTORS GETTING THE BIGGEST PAYCHECKS."

One big expense was marketing. The company constantly tried to find new ways to let people know about Hulu to increase the number of subscribers. But the biggest expense was the production of original content. Expenses are enormous for just one show. Cast and crew need to be paid, with actors getting the biggest paychecks. At this time, Hulu was producing dozens of original series.

One original series that gained significant attention was *11.22.63*, a miniseries based on a novel by Stephen King, which received an Emmy nomination in 2016. Likewise, *Triumph's Election Special 2016* also earned an Emmy nod—marking the first-ever Emmy nominations for Hulu. This helped establish Hulu as a serious player in entertainment.

The success of *The Handmaid's Tale* in 2017 further bolstered Hulu's reputation. A key factor was its weekly release schedule—contrasting with other stream-

Nielsen TV Ratings

For decades, the Nielsen company tracked viewership habits on broadcast and cable/satellite television. These ratings helped determine which shows were most popular. The more popular a show, the more it could charge for advertisements. Almost ten years after Hulu debuted, Nielsen decided to factor Hulu Live TV into its ratings system. As more and more people turned to streaming services, Nielsen decided it needed a fuller picture of what people were watching. Nielsen could track Hulu views across devices, whether people watched it on a television, a smart phone, or computer.

ing services that opted for binge releases, which often see initial spikes in viewership that quickly taper off. This strategy helped *The Handmaid's Tale* maintain steady popularity throughout its two-month season.

In addition to the success of its original programming, Hulu announced in 2017 that it would start offering live TV. For $39.99 per month, subscribers received access to more than 50 TV channels, including news, sports, and entertainment. Those same subscribers also received access to Hulu's large catalog of TV shows and movies. Unlike cable or satellite packages,

"BY LATE 2019, ABOUT 30 MILLION PEOPLE SUBSCRIBED TO HULU."

Hulu subscribers could watch live TV anywhere on a mobile device with internet access. This helped set Hulu apart from the competition. Other services like DirecTV Now, Sling TV, PlayStation Vue, and YouTube TV also offered live TV packages.

The combination of live TV and original programming yielded the results Hulu executives wanted. By late 2019, about 30 million people subscribed to Hulu. However, significant shifts in viewership ensued in

The COVID-19 Pandemic increased subscribers to streaming services

2020. By March, COVID 19 had forced millions to work and attend school remotely, positioning Hulu as a crucial source of entertainment for those with limited options.

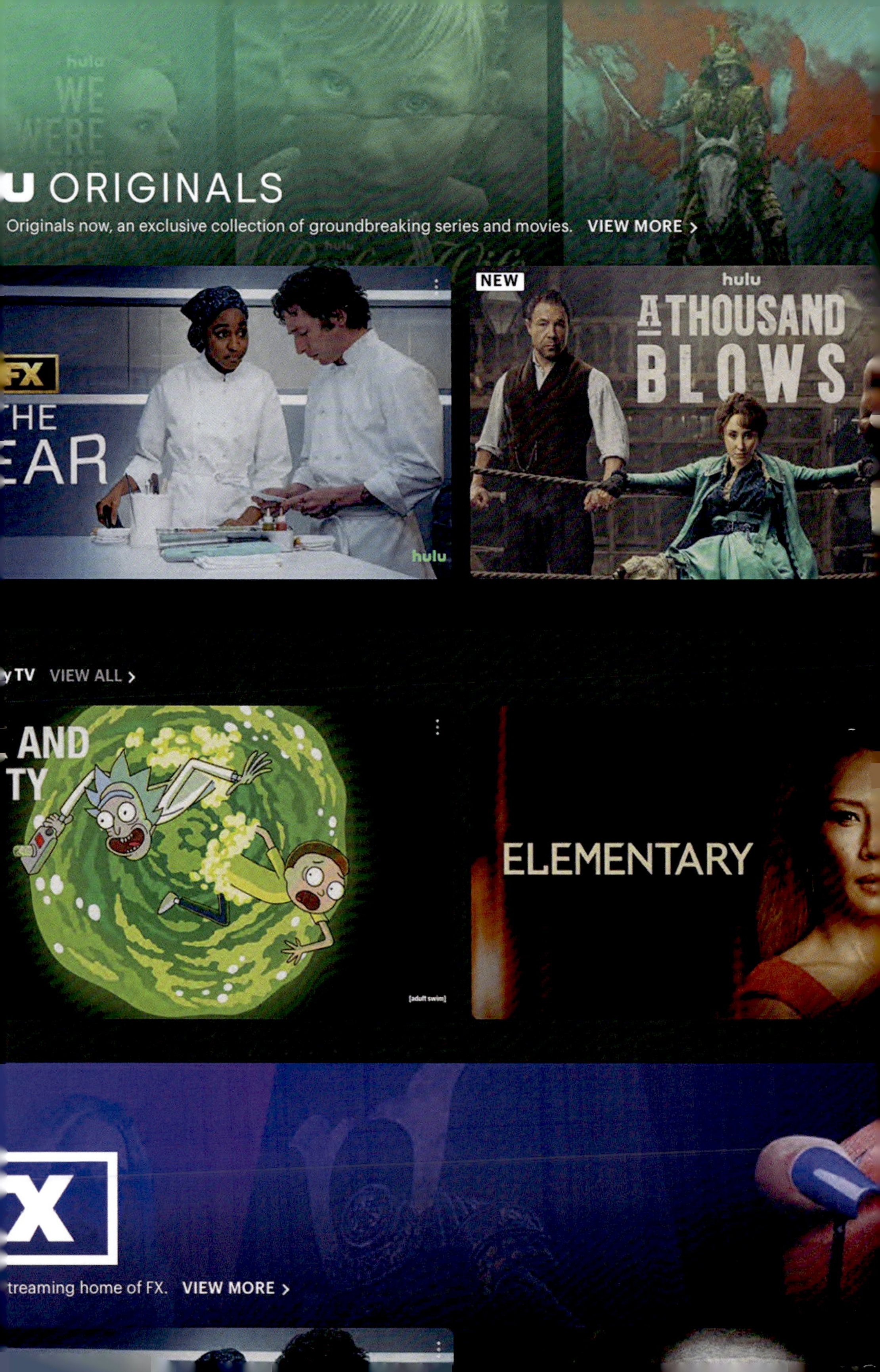
hulu
U ORIGINALS
Originals now, an exclusive collection of groundbreaking series and movies. VIEW MORE >
NEW
hulu
A THOUSAND BLOWS
FX
HE
EAR
hulu
y TV VIEW ALL >
AND
TY
[adult swim]
ELEMENTARY
X
treaming home of FX. VIEW MORE >

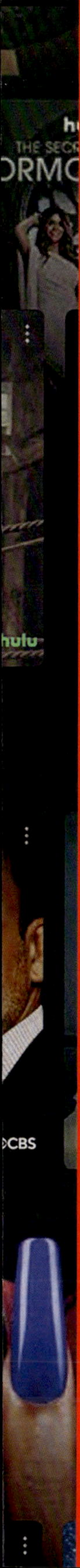

Still Successful After All These Years

All streaming services, including Hulu, saw increased numbers of viewers during the first months of the pandemic. Hulu's subscription numbers increased roughly 30 percent over 2019, going from 28 million to 36.6 million subscribers. The pandemic changed how people watched TV. Instead of subscribing to expensive cable or satellite packages, viewers were likely to subscribe to more than one streaming service. By the end of 2020, households subscribed on average to three streaming services.

OPPOSITE: Hulu now offers many original programs alongside content from other providers.

OPPOSITE A Hollywood advertisement showcases the partnership between Hulu, Disney, and ESPN.

A recent change to Hulu's ownership structure offered customers something new. Notably, in 2019, Disney gained full control of Hulu and became the majority owner. This struck a major blow to Netflix. Disney pulled many of its popular movies, like *Lilo & Stitch* and *Star Wars*, from Netflix and put them on Hulu. Disney already dominated the sports-fan market with ESPN+, and in late 2019 it launched Disney+ to offer more kids' programming. Now that it fully controlled Hulu, Disney targeted adult subscribers seeking general comedies and dramas.

Hulu also became the first streaming company to offer its services as **bundles**. When Disney+ launched in November 2019, customers could add on Hulu and ESPN+ for one price of $12.99. This option positioned Hulu as a major competitor to the larger Netflix. Some

STEPHEN A's WORLD
REAM
BIG.
THE HANDMAID'S TALE
THE DISNEY BUNDLE
lu
Disney+
ESPN+
ONLY $13.99/MONTH
TheDisneyBundle.com

OPPOSITE Competition between streaming services encouraged each one to create more original content.

analysts even thought that Netflix would lose subscribers. Experts expected that people who wanted Disney programming would switch to the Hulu bundle. But the pandemic boosted all streaming services. The prediction that Hulu would gain ground on Netflix never came true.

Hulu kept expanding its offerings, even as people and kids returned to work and school. In early 2021, CBS agreed to broadcast its shows on Hulu Live, which made all four major broadcast networks available on the service. Later that year, ESPN+ and Disney+ were added

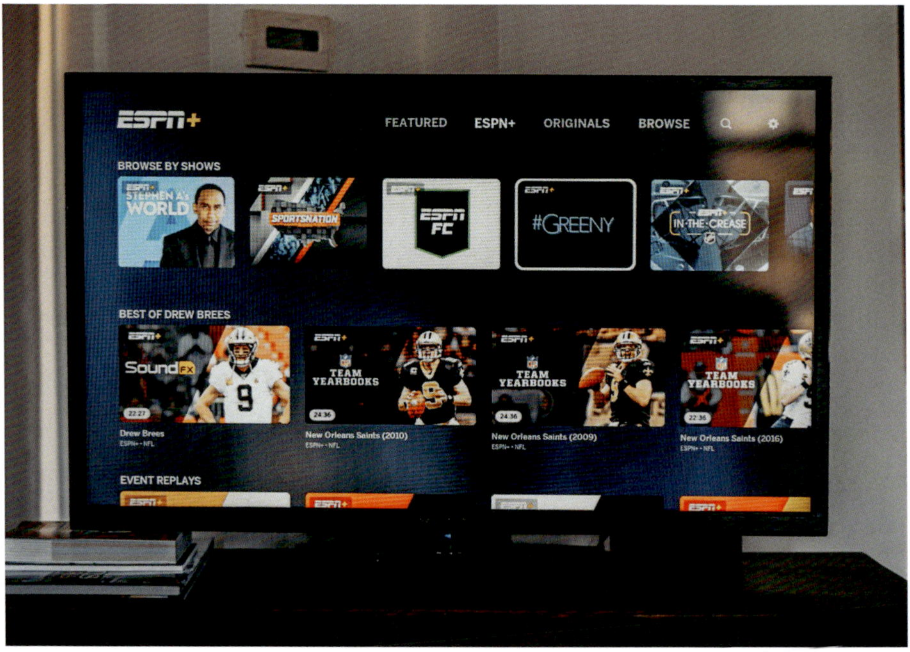

to the Hulu Live lineup. Subscription rates went up by $5, but customers now had 75 channels to choose from.

The corporate structure of Hulu continued to change. In 2023, Disney opted to buy out Comcast and become sole owner of Hulu. On the heels of this news, Hulu announced another bundling option for customers. This

"IN 2023, DISNEY OPTED TO BUY OUT COMCAST AND BECOME SOLE OWNER OF HULU."

time, Max (formerly HBO Max) was included with Hulu and Disney +. Separately, Disney+, Hulu, and Max combined approached Netflix's subscriber numbers. Hulu remained competitive in the streaming wars.

But as always, Hulu's ownership looked for ways to increase profits. Password-sharing was one major problem faced by streaming services like Hulu. Account holders were sharing passwords with people outside of their households, sometimes with several people at once.

OPPOSITE Account sharing has been an issue for all streaming services.

Under terms of agreements in early 2024, Hulu users agreed not to share passwords with people outside of their households. Disney, Hulu's majority owner, reported losses in the millions in 2023 and part of that could be attributed to people accessing Hulu for free.

Hulu and other streaming services faced another troublesome trend by early 2024. Rising prices for goods like groceries and gas stretched budgets thin. People looked to save money wherever they could. Many people took a closer look at what they were paying for stream-

Create a New Profile

PROFILE NAME

Profile Name

KIDS

Turn on to watch only kid-friendly programming

BIRTHDATE ⓘ

Month | Day | Year

GENDER ⓘ

What best describes you?

CREATE PROFILE

CANCEL

Left to right: Ron Meyer, Brian Roberts, CEO of Comcast and Bob Iger, Chairman and CEO of Disney

Negotiations Stall

Disney announced in 2023 that it was buying out Comcast to become sole owner of Hulu. Disney owned two-thirds of the company, while Comcast owned one-third. The two sides have had trouble agreeing on the terms of the sale. Analysts hired by Disney valued Hulu at $27.5 billion. But Comcast's team said it was worth $40 billion. An independent analyst will come up with an unbiased value in hopes the two sides can agree on it. This long process shows how complex large business deals can become.

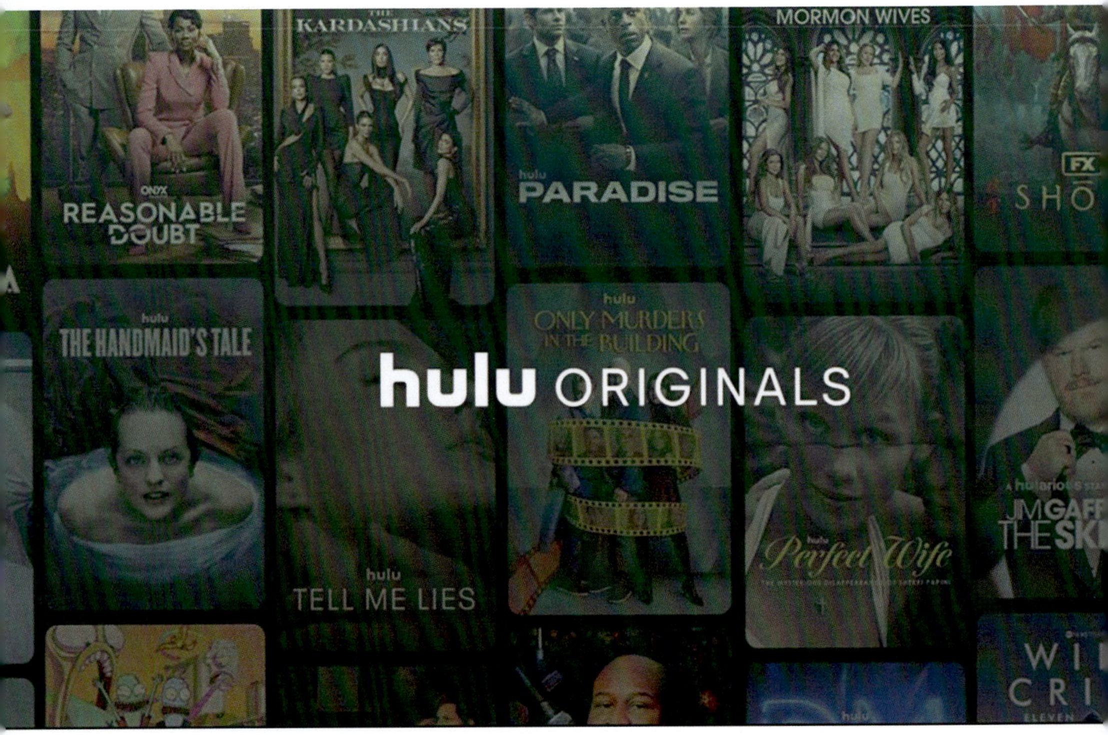

ing services. During the pandemic, households added multiple streaming services because they had time to watch TV at home. But, with people back to work and school, they realized they could save money by cutting back on subscriptions. About 25 percent of subscribers had canceled at least three streaming services in 2023 and 2024. This loss pushed Hulu to find new, creative ways to attract audiences.

By 2025, Hulu's strength remained where it had started almost 20 years before: access to thousands of popular television shows, both current and past. Viewers still can watch shows either as they air live on networks or within 24 hours. Many streaming experts call Hulu a smart choice for its competitive pricing and extensive catalog of TV shows and movies.

If the streaming wars were a horse race with a single winner, Netflix and Amazon Prime might be considered the frontrunners. Yet streaming services actually resemble a pie, with each service offering a unique slice of content. Even without the massive subscriptions or revenue of Netflix or Amazon, Hulu's loyal customers find its endless TV shows, hit movies, and original series hard to beat. Success in innovation is all about finding a **niche**, and Hulu has proved it has found its audience.

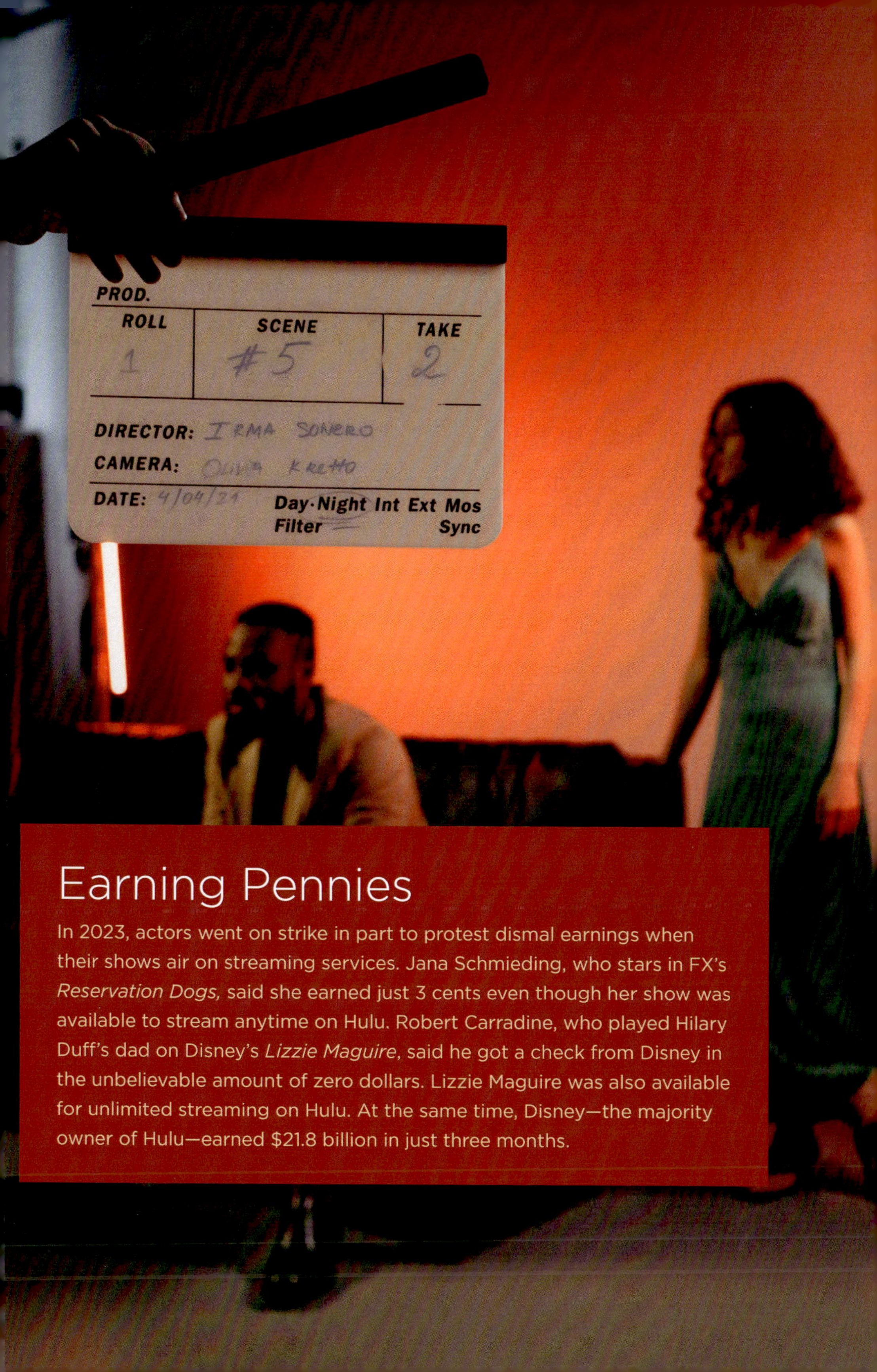

Earning Pennies

In 2023, actors went on strike in part to protest dismal earnings when their shows air on streaming services. Jana Schmieding, who stars in FX's *Reservation Dogs*, said she earned just 3 cents even though her show was available to stream anytime on Hulu. Robert Carradine, who played Hilary Duff's dad on Disney's *Lizzie Maguire*, said he got a check from Disney in the unbelievable amount of zero dollars. Lizzie Maguire was also available for unlimited streaming on Hulu. At the same time, Disney—the majority owner of Hulu—earned $21.8 billion in just three months.

Selected Bibliography

Barnhart, Aaron (ed.). *The Primetimer Guide to Streaming TV.* Hollywood, CA: Primetimer Ventures, 2022.

Daniel, Victor. "As Hulu Live Is Introduced, a Look at TV Streaming Services." *New York Times (Online)*. May 3, 2017.

Krause, Reinhardt. "Hulu in the Red As It Mounts Netflix Challenge." *Investors Business Daily*. November 6, 2015.

Sanson, Kevin and Gregory Steirer. "Hulu, Streaming, and the Contemporary Television Ecosystem." *Media, Culture, and Society*, 2019.

Schechner, Sam, and Elizabeth Holmes. "Disney Climbs Aboard Video Site Hulu, Teaming Up With Other Networks Online." *The Wall Street Journal.* May 1, 2009.

Glossary

antenna a rod or wire that can receive or send television signals.

broadcast to send out through signals that are received through radio or television

broadcast networks TV channels that are relayed to houses over public airwaves.

bundles two or more services packaged together.

cable A way to receive television signal through underground wires that come into homes and connect to a television set.

canceled a TV show that will not be renewed for another season.

digital video discs (DVDs) small, round objects that contain movies or TV shows.

digital video recorders (DVRs) a device that can record a TV program to be watched later.

modem a device connected to a computer that can connect to the internet.

niche a small, specialized audience.

original programming

TV shows or movies that are created by a content provider.

revenue money that a company earns.

satellites objects that orbit the earth in space and transmit signals into people's homes.

start-ups new companies, generally in the technology sector, that begin from the ground-up.

stream to broadcast something over the internet.

tagline a phrase that is associated with a company or group.

video cassette recorders (VCRs)

devices that record a program to save for later that were popular in the 1980s and early 1990s. They also could play movies when a videotape was inserted.

user-generated content

programs that are created by individuals and posted online.

Websites

Hulu
https://www.hulu.com/welcome
Hulu's website for streaming movies and TV shows

What is Hulu and How Does It Work?
https://www.lifewire.com/what-is-hulu-4783546
Learn facts and new information about Hulu and how it works

"Hulu." Britannica.com.
https://www.britannica.com/topic/Hulu
A breakdown of Hulu and it's services

Index